Mies van der Rohe

Mies van der Rohe

Werner Blaser

with 54 photographs, 72 plans and sketches

Thames and Hudson
London

Published in Great Britain in 1972 by Thames and Hudson Ltd, London;
adapted from *Mies van der Rohe: the Art of Structure*, published in 1965.

© 1965 and 1972 Artemis Verlag und Verlag für Architektur, Zürich

Printed in Switzerland

ISBN 0 500 340501 clothbound
      0 500 270201 paperbound

Contents

Foreword

This book, originally published in 1965 and now revised and re-issued in smaller format, took shape during a number of conversations I was privileged to have with Mies van der Rohe in the impressive surroundings of his study in Chicago in 1963 and 1964. Our aim was to set forth the essential ideas underlying the development of the structural forms of his buildings.

There was 'construction' in the very way Mies van der Rohe thought, acted and talked. He did not design. In a slow and profound process of maturation he evolved the structure of each building, analysed it in many detailed sketches, studied each element in his mind and sought out its potentialities and limitations until it could be fitted into the whole. Each step in the process was carried out not only in drawings but also in models; plan and model were thus intimately related.

Mies van der Rohe attached great importance to the workshop in his office. Here proportion, construction and the appearance of the materials were assessed on a model. Extreme care was taken with these models — a drawing cannot convey adequately the rhythm of a steel skeleton, and here a model must decide.

The examples of Mies van der Rohe's work given in this book have been arranged chronologically by types so as to show the development of his architecture. Illustrations and explanations are given of the basic ideas which Mies van der Rohe pursued throughout his life, and for this reason we confined ourselves to the most important buildings. I took new photographs of the buildings in America with the intention of showing their structural development.

The dates in the complete list of works and in the table of contents indicate the year in which each project commenced and (where appropriate) the year of completion of a building. All the texts were originally written in German. Besides giving a description of the buildings — limited to the most essential data on position, construction, materials and dimensions — I have also attempted to sketch Mies van der Rohe's basic philosophy such as he passed on to his associates and pupils as a kind of education in architecture. The quotations scattered throughout the book come from his diaries and from our conversations.

W.B., Basle, 1971

Introduction

Mies van der Rohe evolved his ideas from the basic principles of construction; hence the form of his buildings is the expression of their structure. This book sets out to show how, in his buildings, Mies van der Rohe made a clearly recognized structure the basis of his construction and thus raised it to the level of an art. This elevation of structure to the level of an art will be illustrated by examples ranging from the simple pattern of a brick wall to the transparent construction of a wall of steel and glass.

Mies van der Rohe himself pointed out that the idea that construction must be the basis of the new architecture was not a novel one. It was in fact the point of departure for modern architecture and found expression in Viollet-le-Duc's 'Entretiens sur l'Architecture', which appeared at the beginning of the 1860s. It demands that purposes should be answered honestly and significantly with the means and constructional methods of the time. For Viollet-le-Duc artistic form was not, as for his contemporaries, the question of a new art independent in itself but rather the result of an organized structure. 'Toute forme, qui n'est pas ordonnée par la structure, doit être repoussée.'

Mies van der Rohe was not interested in inventing new forms; rather, by thinking in terms of construction and technology, his aim was to evolve a clear and simple structure. Amidst the confusion of the 'eternally new' in which we live, it is an accomplishment to settle on a consistent form of construction, for, within the scope of a sound and perfected structure, so many variations are possible. He expressed this idea in these words: 'It is absurd to invent arbitrary forms, historical and modernistic forms, which are not determined by construction, the true guardian of the spirit of the times.' He believed this concentration on structure could help the architect in his task.

From the very outset Mies van der Rohe's designs were lucid and uncompromising statements of the idea that a clear distinction was to be made between structural and non-structural elements. It was in the Barcelona Pavilion (1929) with its overlapping, non-bearing walls of fine materials, that structure was raised to a perfect work of art. With it a new period of architecture began. Material, structure, space and the restless need for metaphysical security were here made one. The interplay of closed and open spaces was not calculated but realized as part of an inner harmony.

Even the layman can feel the perfect artistry with which Mies van der Rohe handled the surface plane and the structural elements in his buildings, and can appreciate how, by his work and teaching, he has enabled us to understand those building systems of the past, such as the Doric order, which have created their own structural order. The refinement of the connection between column and roof-slab in the New National Gallery (1963–68) in West Berlin helps us — by the very fact of its being different — to understand the structures of past epochs.

Mies van der Rohe believed that architecture was bound neither to the day nor to eternity, but to the epoch. Only a genuine historical movement makes it what it is. Architecture is the interpretation of a happening in history, the genuine consummation of its inner movement, the fulfilment and expression of its essential nature. In his buildings he sought to express the significant driving forces of our era: the economic order in which we live, the discoveries of science and technology, the existence of the mass society.

In the skeleton-type skyscraper with its glass skin, the curtain wall is raised to the highest level of art and expressed down to the smallest structural detail. The structure in Mies van der Rohe's work determines the entirely flexible arrangement of the plan; and its refinement and classicism are most clearly expressed in the spacious column-free interiors of these one-room buildings where every kind of function can be accommodated.

Mies van der Rohe's final aim was order and truth, a practical beauty which serves mankind. This spiritual order was defined by Thomas Aquinas as *adaequatio rei et intellectus*. It was precisely this truth which was so firmly rooted in the mind of Mies van der Rohe and in every detail of his work. To appreciate this fully takes time; it presupposes that we are ready to penetrate to the heart of solutions which have been distilled to the ultimate in simplicity. Mies van der Rohe performed the meritorious service of redirecting architecture along the path to a deeper spiritual plane and thus to an ultimate unity. Through his work we are able to recognize the spiritual nature of architectural problems and find ever new solutions for them in creative freedom.

Mies van der Rohe:
A personal statement by the architect, 1964

It was about 1910 that I first realized I was embarking on my profes-
sional career. At that time the Jugendstil and Art Nouveau movements
had run their course. Buildings designed to be worthy representatives
of their owners were influenced to a greater or lesser extent by Palladio
and Schinkel. But it was the industrial and other purely technical
buildings that were the greatest achievements of the period. Those were
confused days in which nobody would venture an answer to questions
about the nature of architecture. Perhaps it was still too early for an
answer. All the same, I posed the question and was determined to find
an answer.
It was only after the war, in the 1920s, that the influence exerted by
technical developments on many aspects of life became increasingly
apparent. We recognized technology to be a civilizing force and one to be
reckoned with.
Advancing technology provided the builder with new materials and more
efficient methods which were often in glaring contrast to our traditional
conception of architecture. I believed, nevertheless, that it would be
possible to evolve an architecture with these means. I felt that it must be
possible to harmonize the old and the new in our civilization. Each of my
buildings was a statement of this idea and a further step in my search for
clarity.
It was my growing conviction that there could be no architecture of our
time without the prior acceptance of these new scientific and technical
developments. I have never lost this conviction. Today, as for a long time
past, I believe that architecture has little or nothing to do with the
invention of interesting forms or with personal inclinations.
True architecture is always objective and is the expression of the inner
structure of our time, from which it stems.

The approach to structure

It was always a distinguishing feature of Mies van der Rohe's work in Germany (before he emigrated to the United States) that he refused to imitate earlier styles and sought single-mindedly for constructions which articulated the material into a clear and visible structure matched to the purpose of the building and the nature of the material itself. Subjective and merely decorative trimmings were shunned and the law of structure strictly obeyed. He designed many projects which were never executed: they were visionary schemes far in advance of their time. This was absolute architecture pointing the way to the future.
Mies van der Rohe concentrated on the properties of his building material and clearly expressed these in his charcoal drawings and model studies. In his first tower projects, for example, glass was not seen in large surfaces but was broken up by angles for the sake of light reflection and the effect of depth. In the brick villa every wall revealed the character of the brickwork down to the smallest detail. It is astonishing to see that, besides this sensitive treatment of material, flexible interlocking spatial patterns and the free-standing load-bearing wall were already featured in the work of this early period. In the reinforced-concrete office building cantilevering was used with convincing skill and a new conception of space created by turning up the floor slabs along their edges. What mattered was invariably the development of structure and constructional possibilities, never arbitrary forms.

Glass skyscraper on a prismatic plan, competition project 1919

The charcoal sketch shows an office skyscraper near the Friedrichstrasse station in Berlin. It is a 20-storey steel skeleton, encased in glass, with one front overlooking the Spree. The triangular shape of the site suggested the prismatic form of the plan. The perspective view clearly shows how the glass surfaces are set at angles so as to fit the outline of the plan and thus produce a rich play of light reflections.

Charcoal drawing:
Glass skyscraper on
a prismatic plan

14

Glass skyscraper on a polygonal plan, project 1920—21

Studies of light reflections on a glass model led to a polygonal plan being adopted. The curves followed by the glass walls were determined by the lighting needs of the interior, by the appearance of the building mass when seen against the existing buildings in the street and by the play of reflections it was desired to achieve.

The two glass skyscrapers were experiments which matured out of one and the same thought process: to exploit the potentialities of the materials and technology of a new age and to create something meaningful out of them.

Reinforced-concrete building, project 1922

In this project for an office building the floors are formed by cantilevered concrete slabs which are turned up and around at the edges. The niches thus formed around the periphery of the building are two metres in height and are used as storage cabinets, thus leaving the interior free and uncluttered. As the ribbon window running round the perimeter is flush with the front of these cabinets, it appears set well back from the façade when viewed from outside. The columns of the concrete skeleton are located four metres back from the façade on all sides. Since each floor is a space, great flexibility is possible in the layout of offices.

Charcoal drawing: Glass skyscraper on a polygonal plan

Charcoal drawing: Project for a block of offices in reinforced concrete with cantilevered floors

Brick villa, project 1923

The garden is divided by three long straight walls of brick. The villa itself
crystallizes around their meeting point. The load-bearing brick walls are
set out as the floor plan requires and connect the interior and exterior.
The various living areas in the interior are screened from one another
and yet there is an easy flow of space from one room to the next. There
are no corridors.

The flat roof rests on walls in which no openings are cut. Simple means
have been used to banish the image of the conventional villa. The plan of
the brick villa is a good example of the way in which Mies van der Rohe
developed the art of structure from the very beginning. The structure of
a brick wall begins with the smallest unit into which the whole can be
divided: the brick. The dimensions are calculated in terms of the brick
as the basic unit.

There has been no essential change in the bonding of a brick wall for
centuries. Mies' discovery was to recognize the fundamental law and logic
of the material and to unify the walls in a well-proportioned interplay
of volumes and open spaces both inside and outside.

Charcoal drawing: Brick as a material for house
and garden walls

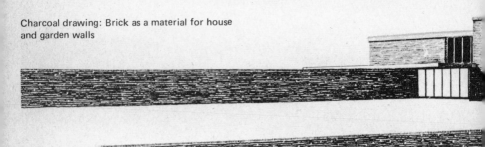

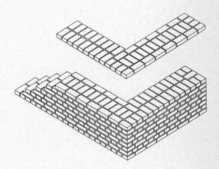

Detail of brick courses

Brick villa, project: plan of free-standing
brick walls

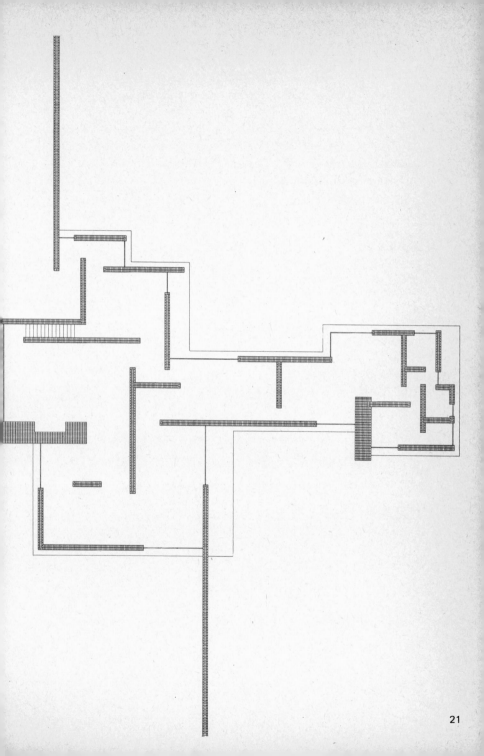

Concrete villa, project 1924

The outer load-bearing walls of the villa were planned as reinforced-concrete slabs. The material allows windows to be cut in the outer wall wherever they are needed. The simple geometrical forms of the façade make the whole look as if it had been cast in a single mould.
The various living areas are independent cubes which are set at angles to each other and form courts or patios. The result is a clearly articulated plan which emphasizes the play of forms between the house, the garden and the natural setting. In the large inner room the roof is supported on columns.

Charcoal drawing of the villa, showing
cantilevered elements and indentations in
the façade

Court houses with steel columns

In court or patio houses the contrast between supporting and supported elements is clearly stated. This design has been largely instrumental in promoting further development towards a flexible plan and the satisfaction of the need for light, air and verdure. The roof is supported on brick walls and an interior system of steel columns. The house and the court are surrounded by brick walls between which are openings; the dimensions of these openings are based on brick modules.

In the German Pavilion at Barcelona Mies van der Rohe first developed non-bearing walls of costly materials arranged with overlapping planes. Here the definition of architecture as *Baukunst* carried special conviction, *Bau* (building) being the static and law-conforming element based on a strict intellectual order, and *Kunst* (art) the free and creative element which can operate within a clear structure.

German Pavilion at the 1929 World Exhibition in Barcelona

On a site at the World Exhibition in Barcelona there was erected an imposing pedestal measuring 53 x 17 metres which the visitor had to traverse. Free-standing walls of fine materials enclosed the pavilion and formed a pattern of open and closed spaces. The pavilion had no function other than to look worthy of the country it represented.

The terrace, surfaced in travertine, was partly occupied by two pools of different sizes. The roof-slab covering part of the remaining area was supported on eight steel columns of cruciform section encased in chromium-plated covers. Honey-coloured golden onyx, green Tinian marble and tinted and frosted glass were employed for the overlapping walls were made. An existing block of onyx was split twice and the resulting slabs, placed one over the other, determined the height of the pavilion (3.10 metres). The only transverse wall to join two others was made of frosted glass and contained lighting which provided diffuse illumination both inside and outside the pavilion. The chairs and stools in the interior were of flat chromium-plated steel bars upholstered with cushions of white leather; the tables were topped with slabs of black opal glass. In the water court, one of the roofless demi-patios, stood a figure of a dancer by Georg Kolbe.

Part of the terrace,
showing travertine
marble slabs (each
approx. 1 metre
square), and walls
independent of the
cruciform load-
bearing columns

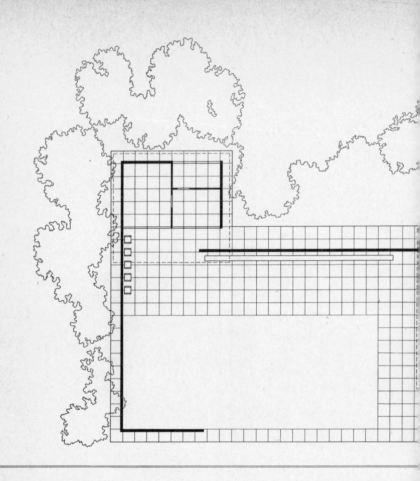

General plan of the Barcelona Pavilion
Overall dimensions, 23 x 53 m

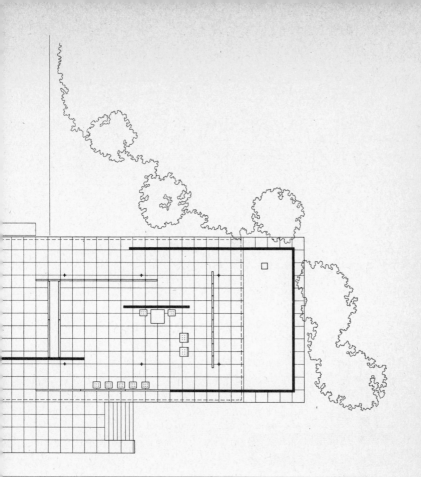

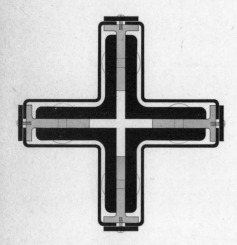

Section of cruciform column. Scale 1:10

General view of terrace, showing roof-slab and▷
walls of stone and glass

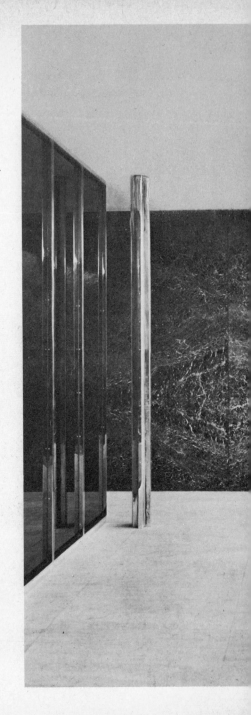

Integration of architecture and fine art in the
water court

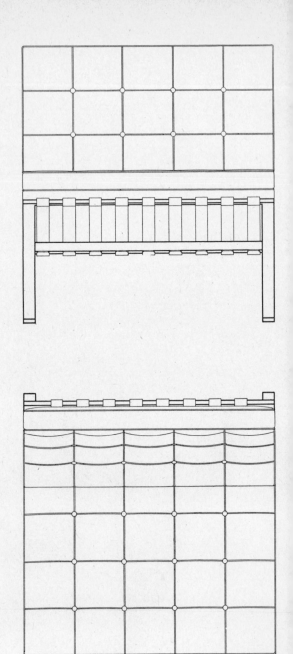

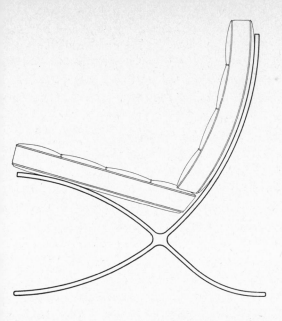

Barcelona chair in steel and leather.
Scale 1:12.5

House in the Alps, project 1934

The sketch was made for the architect's own house in a mountain resort. The interior rooms are defined by walls and large areas of glass. An inner court provides protection from the wind and a link between inside and outside.

Spanning a valley depression, the house grows out of the landscape. Mountain and house are one: 'The mountain is my house.'

Charcoal drawing: House in the Alps

House with three courts, project 1934

This living area for a family is enclosed by a brick wall of full storey height around its perimeter. Part of the area is covered with a roof-slab which, supported on slim steel columns, rests upon the brick wall. The system of supports in the interior allows the room to be subdivided as desired. The living rooms can be opened on all sides into the garden, with which they form a pleasing harmony.
These court houses are admirably suited to urban living conditions. Within an enclosure that excludes all extraneous disturbance, one can live in rooms of choice simplicity, where indoors and outdoors are harmoniously related.

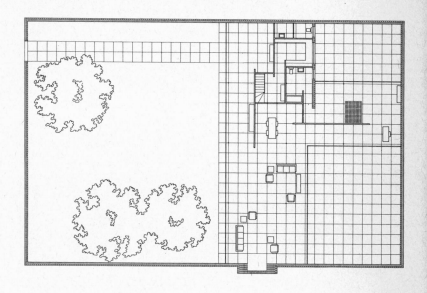

Elevation and plan of the court house
Scale 1:400

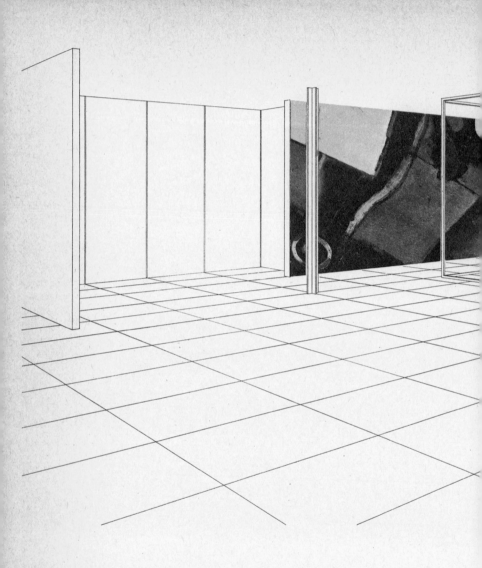

House with three courts, collage with
composition by Georges Braque

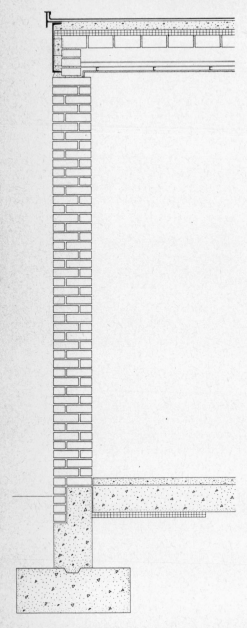

Court house: vertical section of load-bearing
wall and detail of roof-slab. Scale 1:30

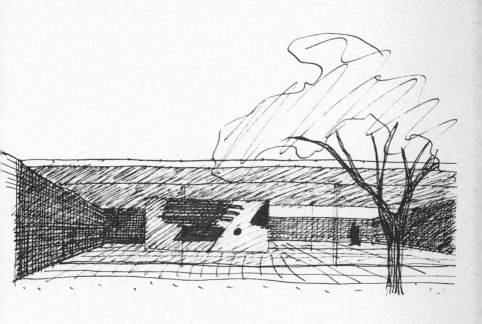

Pen-and-ink sketch: view through a court
house (1934)

Load-bearing steel columns with glass wall
behind. View into the walled court

Group of court houses, project 1931

The rectangular site is screened from the outside world by a brick wall around its perimeter. Three properties, each of different size, are partitioned off by walls.
All the walls are set on the lines of a planning grid in which the module is a brick. Part of each court is covered by a roof-slab under which the rooms flow one into the other. The various living areas open into secluded courts. In these houses all the enclosed space indoors and outdoors is used as a living area.
In a town-planning scheme a district of court houses forms a residential zone consisting of circumscribed living areas each with its own intimate atmosphere. The houses are, as it were, cloisters in which the individual can live in complete privacy.

Plan showing part of a development of court houses and public access roads.
Scale approx. 1:1,200

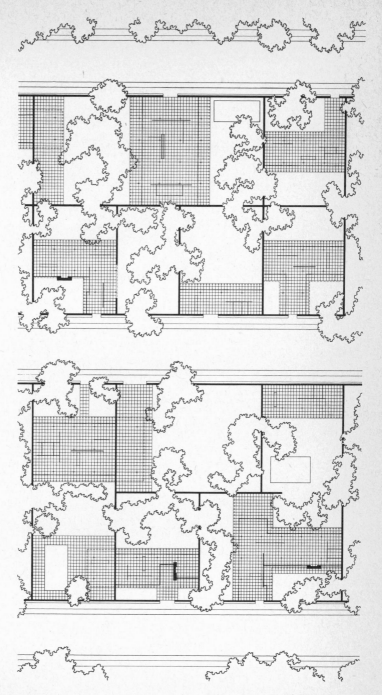

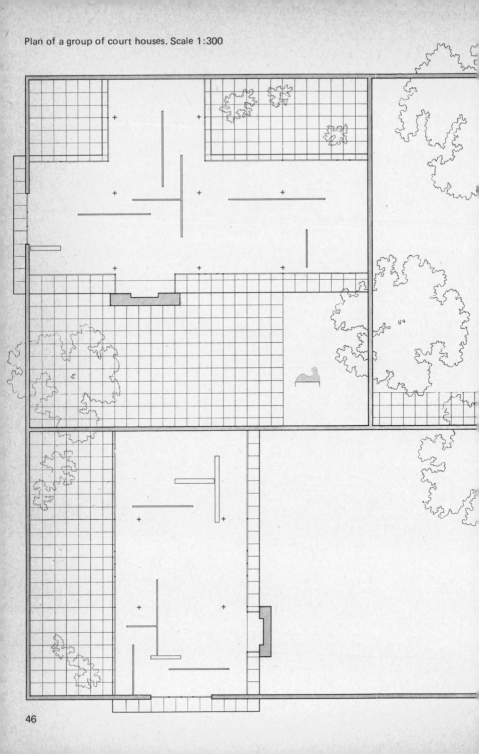

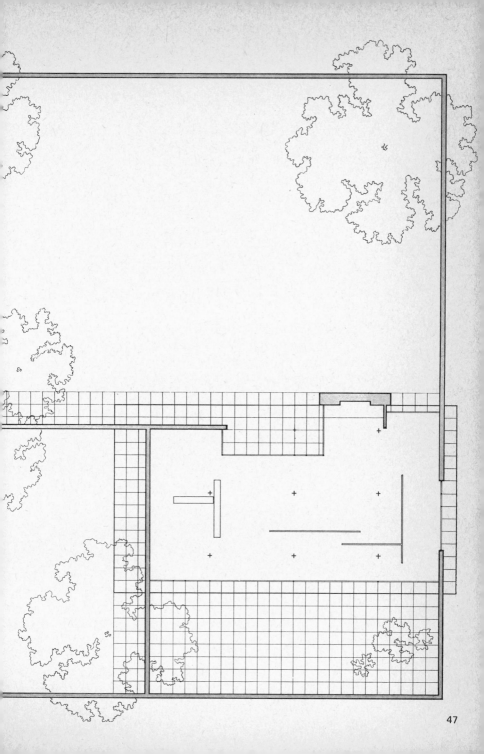

Mies van der Rohe:
Principles of Architectural Education

The school of architecture has two aims: to train the architect by imparting the necessary knowledge and skills, and to educate him in order that he can make proper use of the knowledge and skills he has acquired. Thus training has practical purposes in view, but education has values. It is the business of education to implant insight and responsibility. It must turn irresponsible opinion into responsible judgment and lead from chance and arbitrariness to the rational lucidity of an intellectual order.

In its simplest forms architecture is rooted in the purely utilitarian but it can reach up through the whole gamut of values into the highest sphere of spiritual existence, into the realm of pure art.

This realization must be the starting point for any system of architectural education. Step by step, it must make clear what is possible, what is necessary and what is significant. This is why the various subjects must be co-ordinated so that there is organic unity at every stage and the student can study all the different aspects of building in their relationships to one another.

Apart from technical instruction, the student should first learn to draw so as to train hand and eye and master his means of expression. Exercises will give him a sense of proportion, structure, form and material and show him how they are related and what they can express. Th student should then get to know the materials and construction of simple buildings in timber, stone and brick, and then go on to find out what can be done with steel and reinforced concrete as building materials. At the same time he should learn how these elements are significantly interrelated and how they are directly expressed in form.

Any material, whether natural or artificial, has its special properties which one must know before one can work with it. New materials and new methods of construction are not necessarily superior. What matters is the way they are handled. The value of a material depends on what we make of it.

After materials and methods of construction, the student must familiarize himself with functions. They must be clearly analysed so that he knows precisely what they involve. It must be clearly understood why and how one building scheme differs from another. What it is that gives it its special character.

Any introduction to the problems of city-planning must teach the fundamentals on which it is based and show clearly how all aspects of building are interconnected and related to the city as an organism. Finally, and by way of a synthesis of the whole course of instruction, the student is introduced to building as an art. He is taught the essential nature of art, the application of its means and its realization in the building.

But these studies must also include an analysis of the spirit of our times upon which we are dependent. Present and past must be compared for differences and similarities in both a material and spiritual sense. This is why the buildings of the past must be studied and vividly described so as to convey a clear grasp of their essentials. It is not merely a matter of taking their greatness and significance as an architectural criterion but also of realizing that they were bound to a particular non-recurrent historical situation and thus place us under a duty to aspire to our own creative achievements.

Illinois Institute of Technology (IIT), Chicago, 1938—58:
Steel-frame campus buildings

The campus of an American university is an area, complete in itself, in which classrooms, research facilities and, for some students, accommodation are provided.

A slum area had to be cleared to make way for the buildings of the new IIT campus. It was a condition imposed by the city that the existing street system should be retained. The area where the campus was to be developed was divided into a planning grid based on a 24-foot module. Limited funds made extreme economy essential and this is reflected in the materials and forms of construction: load-bearing brick walls, exposed reinforced-concrete skeletons and pure steel skeletons filled with brick or glass. The beauty of materials and the masterly skill with which they are handled architecturally show to particular advantage in the single-storey buildings where it was not necessary to fireproof the structure with concrete. The design of the classroom and laboratory blocks was based on a lucid order and structure and has not been outdated by the passage of time — although the campus took twenty-five years to build.

The buildings on the IIT campus are particularly clear examples of the skin and skeleton type of construction. This principle affords the greatest possible freedom in the design of the plan and façade. The load-bearing structural parts provide, as it were, the skeleton while the walls filling the gaps form the skin. The idea is in itself centuries old.

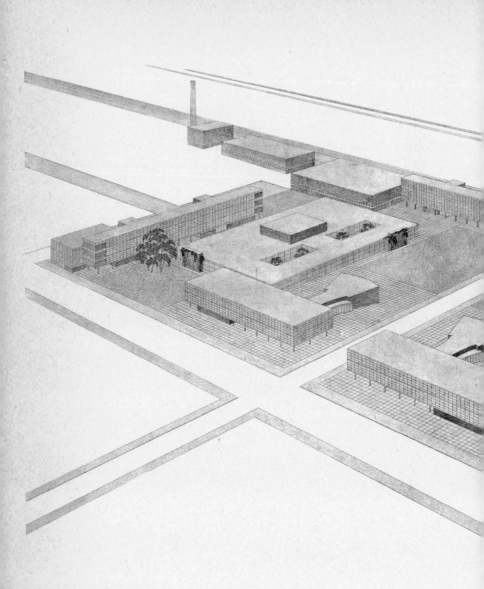

Illinois Institute of Technology: Original project

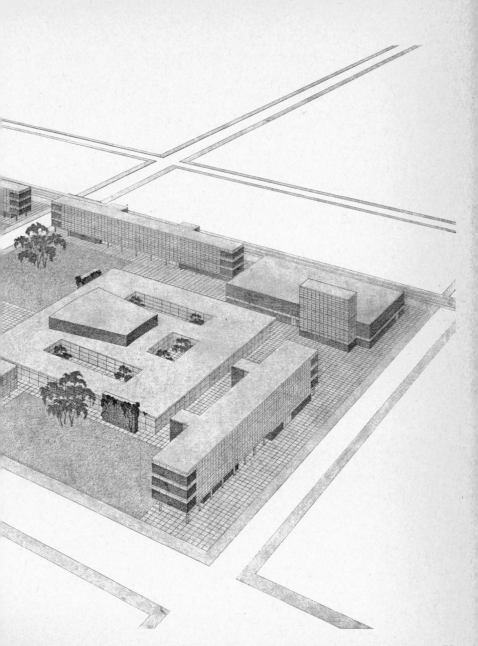

Chemical Engineering and Metallurgy Building (IIT) 1945

The programme of the Chemical Engineering and Metallurgy Building called for a two-storey building 5 modules by 12 modules on plan (campus module 24 x 24 feet).
The structural parts of this steel-framed building are fireproofed with concrete. The skin is stepped forward one brick length in front of the outer edge of the columns. An I-beam is welded to the column. The brick wall forming the panel is keyed in between its flanges. Outside it is flush with the front edge of the rolled-steel section. At parapet height a T-section caps the wall and is tied into the centre of the top course of stretchers. The space remaining between the vertical load-bearing sections and the steel facing of the floor-slab, whose surface is flush with the vertical I-beam, is closed with a glass window in a steel frame. The steel window-frame and the panel wall are set off from the vertical I-beam and the upper edge of the steel facing of the floor-slab by a visible joint. The contrast between the non-bearing wall and the bearing stanchions is particularly evident at the corner of the building. Trees shade the glazing which runs the full length of the façade, behind which the classrooms and laboratories are located. The rooms of the teaching staff are arranged around an inner court.

The main entrance is an integral part of the ▷ façade

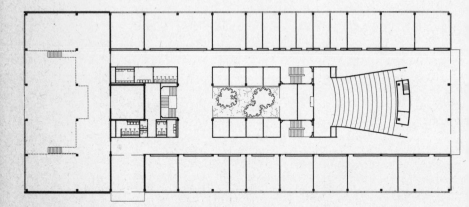

Chemical Engineering and Metallurgy
Building: plan showing classrooms around
inner court and auditorium. Scale 1:800

Side entrance showing aluminium-framed ▷
double doors on swivel hinges

Chemistry Building, IIT, 1945
Alumni Memorial Hall, 1945

These two buildings are of fireproof steel-frame construction. The exposed parts of the frame are painted black and the panels are filled with sand-coloured bricks and glass.

Variations in the number of floors and in the dimensions, which are always based on the module, make for harmony in the disposition of the buildings over the site plan. The trees, planted at the time of construction, soften the strict rhythms of the façades. Wild ivy adds a lively touch to the large areas of brick wall and forms an attractive contrast to the precision of the technical forms.

The details of the glass-and-steel skeleton buildings of IIT are more or less identical. In plan and elevation the proportions of the Alumni Memorial Hall are particularly pleasing and harmonious.

Inner garden court of the Chemical
Engineering and Metallurgy Building

Pencil drawing: Alternative plan for siting
buildings

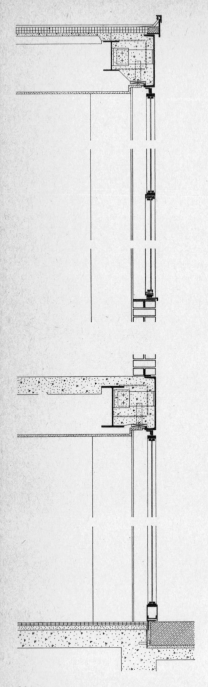

Typical vertical section. Scale approx. 1:30

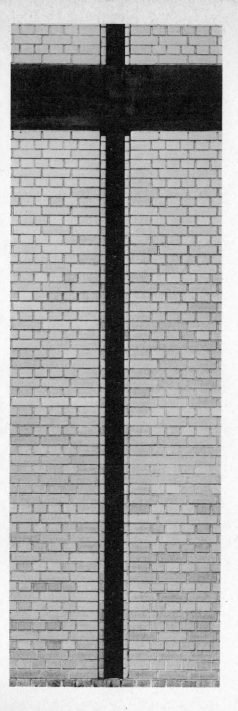

Detail of external wall, showing brickwork
recessed at junction with steel I-beam

Chemistry Building: general view of façade ▷
showing symmetrical pattern

65

Typical horizontal section. Scale 1:25

Detail of steel frame and brickwork with ivy ▷
growth

The east façade of the two-storey Alumni ▷▷
Memorial Hall

Library and administration building, IIT, 1944

This, the most mature project among the campus buildings, unfortunately will never be built. When Mies van der Rohe retired from teaching at the IIT, the administration no longer felt under an obligation to have his projects executed.

Because the library and administration building was in the form of a one-storey hall the regulation calling for a fireproof casing over the structural steelwork of multi-storey buildings did not apply. Features of construction such as the transfer of loads to stanchions and the junction of surfaces of different materials are clearly visible both inside and outside. All the constructional elements employed are subordinated to the load-bearing steel structure.

The hall is 13 modules long (312 feet) and 28 feet high. It is 8 modules (192 feet) wide with a column every third module. The offices along the two long sides of the hall are subdivided by means of partitions 8 feet high. The book-stack of the library is enclosed from ground-level to the roof line by brick walls. A mezzanine platform — set aside for the administration — is held between four inside columns and overlooks the interior court.

The I-beam, which is a particularly prominent feature of this library, can be stressed in only one direction. This, Mies van der Rohe referred to as the Gothic principle — the column which is cruciform or star-shaped in cross-section and can be loaded in two directions being typical of the Renaissance.

Detail of the proposed girder construction

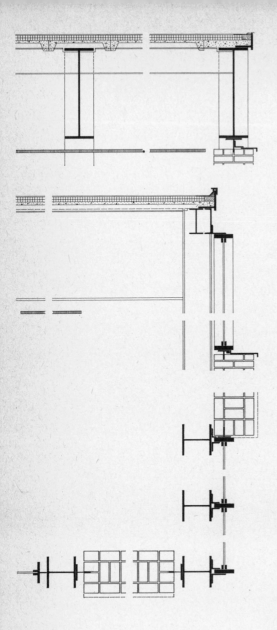

The use of the steel I-beam: details of two
vertical sections (above) and one horizontal
section. Scale approx. 1:35

Corner detail showing combination of
building materials and method of construction

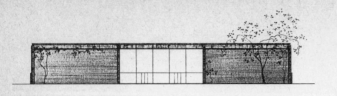

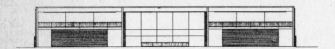

Library and administration building: south
and north elevations, and (below) cross-sections
showing stairs to mezzanine platform and full-
height brick walls enclosing library book-stacks
Scale 1:800

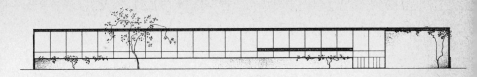

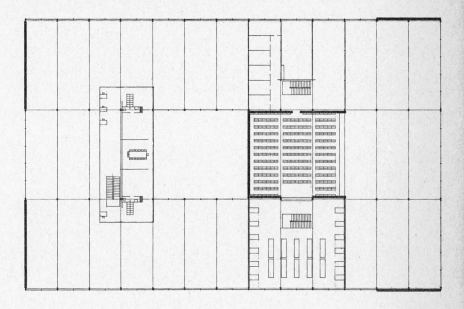

Front (east) elevation and (below) plan at
mezzanine level. Scale 1:800

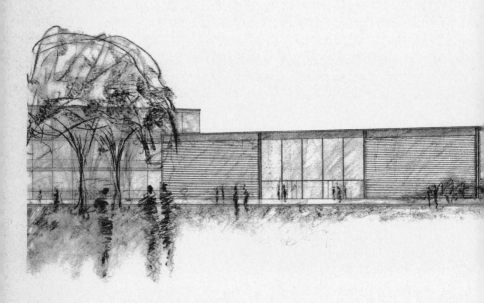

Sketch showing the proposed library and
administration building in its setting

Truss construction with suspended roof

With the aim of providing complete flexibility of arrangement in the
interior, a vast hall-like structure entirely free of internal columns has
been created at IIT. The roof is suspended from a system of trusses which
are supported upon outside columns, thus leaving the interior entirely
unobstructed. The interior of the building is simply a large space enclosed
by the flat suspended roof and the vertical outer skin of glass. It
therefore achieves the ultimate in unity of spatial, aesthetic and
technological organization. Mies van der Rohe said: 'Where technology
attains its true fulfilment, it transcends into architecture.'
This system of truss construction for large halls can serve a variety of
functions.

Crown Hall (IIT): Architecture and Design Building, 1950–56

This glass-and-steel hall, which is free from inside supports, provides a
work centre for the students and staff of the faculty of architecture
and town planning (working together in such close proximity makes for
an easy relationship between students and benefits their studies).
Students' work is regularly on display in the central exhibition area of
the hall.
The roof of the building measures 120 x 220 feet. It is suspended from
four welded plate-girders which span the entire width of the roof at
60-foot centres. At the ends the roof-slab projects 20 feet beyond the
outer truss. A glass-and-steel wall encloses the building. The lower panels
of glass are sand-blasted; the upper windows and those at the entrance
are of transparent glass; fitted on the inside above the sand-blasted glass
are venetian blinds which are kept in a down position to ensure an even
distribution of light. A monumental flight of travertine steps leads
by way of a platform terrace to the main entrance level, which is 6 feet
above the ground. The white acoustic ceiling is 18 feet above the terrazzo
floor. The free-standing partitions are of oak.

Post and beam as structural elements

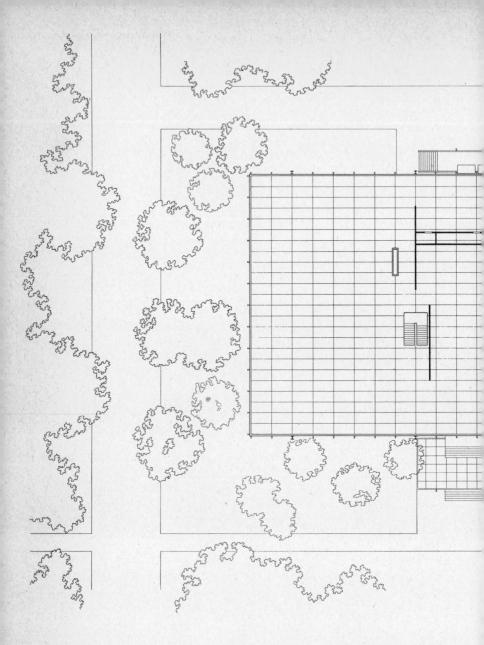

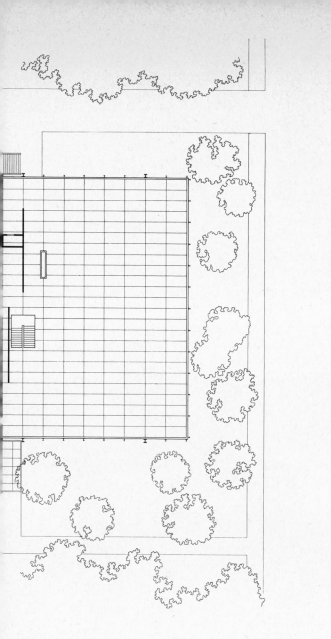

General plan of Crown Hall. Scale 1:500

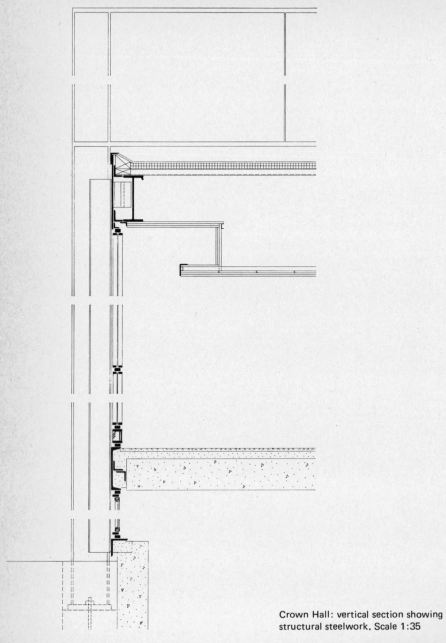

Crown Hall: vertical section showing
structural steelwork. Scale 1:35

Crown Hall under construction: the principal plate girders are at 60-ft centres and span the entire width of the building

General view showing steps leading to main ▷ entrance. The stark lines of the building are softened by the surrounding trees

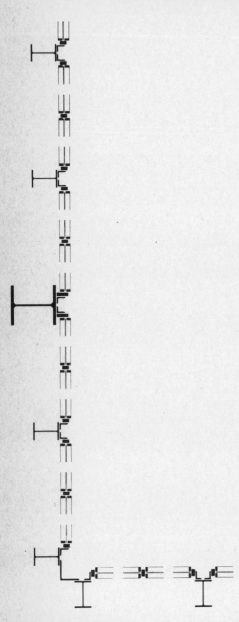

Crown Hall: horizontal section showing use
of steel columns. Scale 1:30

The platform and steps leading to the main ▷
entrance as seen from within

Crown Hall: main entrance with entrance steps
in travertine marble

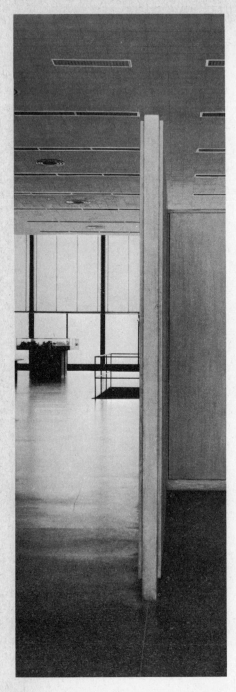

Crown Hall: typical movable partition in oak

General view of interior showing use of wooden▷
partitions

Crown Hall: view from within, showing steel columns, sand-blasted glass panels and venetian blinds in permanent down position

National Theatre, Mannheim, competition entry, 1952—53

This project consists of a low, transparent hall in which are incorporated a large theatre for 1,300 persons and a small theatre for 500 persons. Visitors enter the building by way of the ground floor which is 4 metres high and set back about 8 metres from the façade. The walls, which are faced with marble, seem to flow through the building. The upper floor is 12 metres high and houses two seating areas, a portion of the larger being cantilevered into the auditorium. The stages share a common area in the centre.

The roof-slab, which is 160 metres long, is suspended from seven lattice trusses which span the 80 metres of the site at centres of 24 metres. The enclosing wall is of steel and glass.

Model of the theatre building, detail showing roof-slab suspended from lattice girders. Part of the cantilevered balcony can be seen within

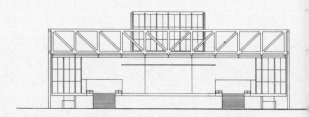

Section of the Mannheim theatre project.
Scale 1:1,200

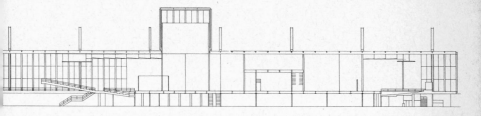

Longitudinal section and plan. Scale 1:1,200

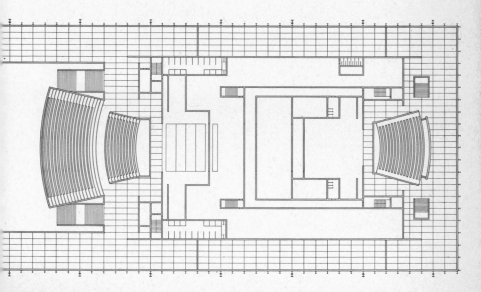

Glass houses with a steel frame

The columns are located outside so as to give infinite flexibility in internal arrangement. The construction of the roof-slab depends on whether the columns are arranged along the two long sides of the house or all round its perimeter.

The use of steel and glass gives an uninterrupted view of the natural surroundings and enables the interior space to be projected outside. A pedestal or terrace in front of the building fits the house harmoniously into its environment.

These steel-and-glass structures are set like crystals amidst the luxuriance of nature. Only the art of omission reveals the true structure of a building and reduces it to elements of pure beauty and pure spirit.

Farnsworth House, Plano (Illinois), 1945–50

This weekend house is an open-planned single-storey building; raised above ground level, it stands in a meadow and is surrounded by tall trees. The living area overlooks the Fox River, which forms the southern limit of the site.

The roof and floor-slab are supported by eight outside columns, the living space being enclosed by a glass skin. An inner core of partitions in natural primavera wood encloses the service installations and separates the kitchen, sleeping and living areas.

A raised terrace in front of the house leads down to ground level, the different levels being joined by two flights of steps. The steps, the terrace and the floor are faced with travertine slabs measuring 2 x 3 feet. All exposed steel elements are painted white. The walls of clear glass can be screened by curtains of natural-coloured shantung. The dimensions of the house are 77 x 29 feet. The pedestal measures 55 x 22 feet and the interior is 9 ft 6 in. high. The columns are placed 22 feet apart.

The house seen from across the Fox River in ▷
winter

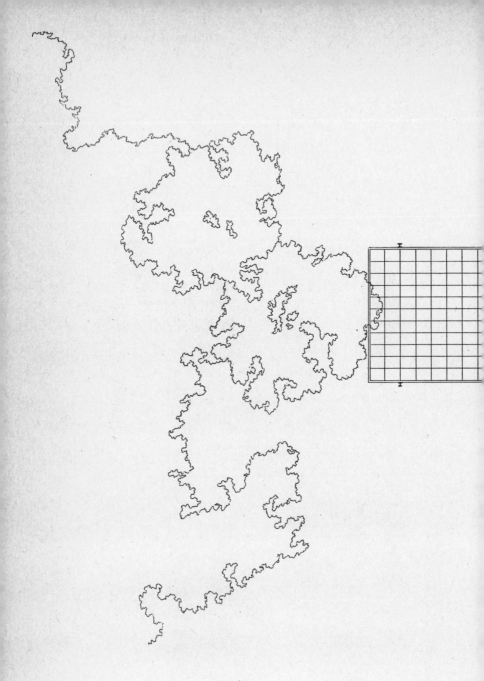

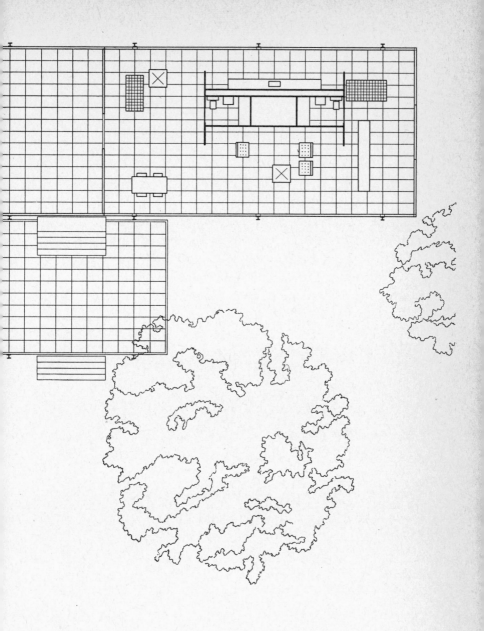

General plan of the Farnsworth house.
Scale 1:200

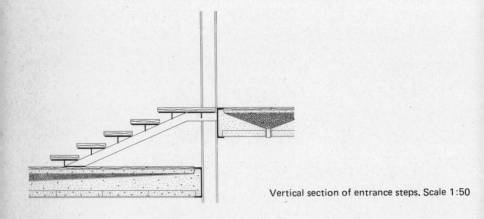

Vertical section of entrance steps. Scale 1:50

The terrace and steps up to the entrance; ▷
paving and floor are of travertine slabs

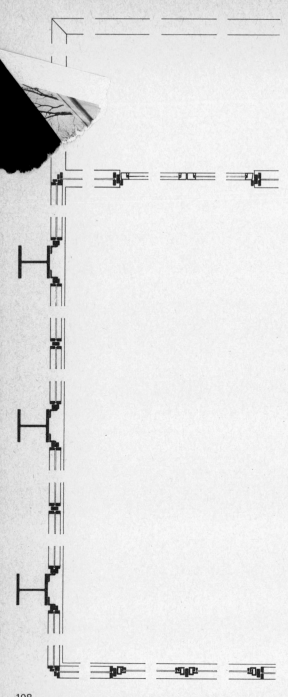

The Farnsworth house: horizontal
section showing external columns,
window frames etc.
Scale 1:25

View from the entrance towards▷
the Fox River. The view of the
landscape from within is
broken only by the window
frames.

General view from the north, ▷▷
showing steel frame painted
white, walls of clear glass, and
natural-coloured shantung
curtains

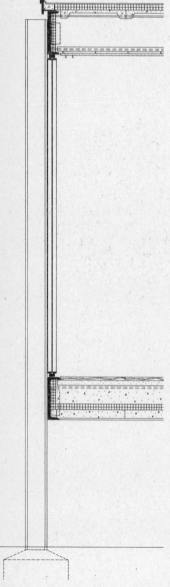

The Farnsworth house: vertical section showing
detail of roof- and floor-slab construction.
Scale 1:35

Detail of standard I-beam column and cornice ▷

Caine House, project 1950

This project was the solution to a building programme to meet a variety of needs at a high level of luxury. The different zones for family life are accommodated under a roof-slab, measuring 48 x 110 feet, supported on 12 steel columns. The floor is of stone slabs planned on a module of 3 x 5 feet, and extends outside to form a terrace. A glass wall around the perimeter of the roof-slab encloses the house itself.
The service rooms and the servants' bedrooms, together with the children's playrooms, are separated from the main part of the house, where free-standing screens divide up the space into living and sleeping areas for the family and guests.

General plan of multi-room glass house; the service area is at the right, and the main living area in the centre. Scale 1:400

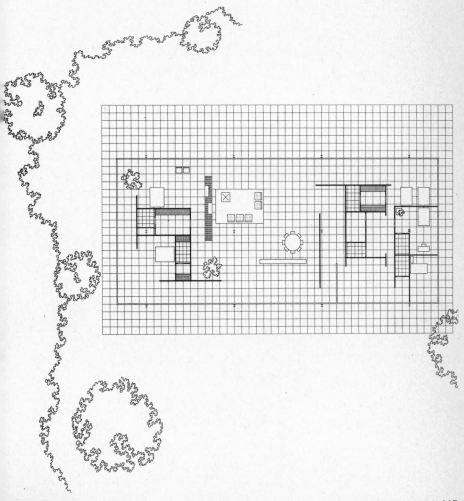

115

Glass house with four columns, project 1950

A square room is open on all four sides. The roof-slab is the only visible horizontal element and appears to hover over the low partition walls. The rigid roof-slab measuring 50 x 50 feet consists of a grid of square steel sections welded together; it is supported on four centrally placed external columns, one on each side of the building. Set aside from the centre, a core containing the plumbing separates the service and the living areas. The basic idea was to situate a house so that it was open in all directions to the surrounding landscape. It is a pavilion in a garden and like the court houses is screened from the road by a brick wall.

General plan of glass house with four columns, the floor slab being extended to form a large terrace. Scale 1:400

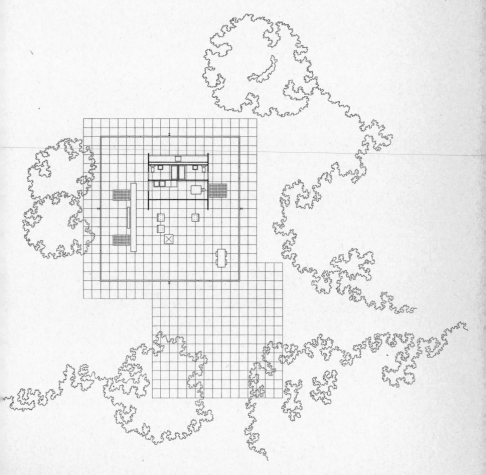

117

Steel-and-glass apartment towers

The first tower blocks of apartments were executed in reinforced concrete. A drawing of the façade in steel and glass showed the way to erecting tower blocks as steel-framed buildings. These buildings are the fruits of research over a quarter of a century. By day and by night their proportions, their patterning and their glass walls make a vivid impression.

The outside sections of rolled steel or extruded aluminium containing the glass form a vigorously articulated main façade. Since the view from inside the apartment is unrestricted, the occupants enjoy an entirely new experience of their environment, with a sense of freedom and detachment.

At the 860 Lake Shore Drive Apartments the I-beams were welded directly to the steel plates which cover the exterior of the fireproofed steel frame. Thus the load-bearing columns and the floor spandrels become visible on the face of the building.

At the 900 Esplanade Apartments and the Commonwealth Promenade Apartments, on the other hand, the window units are placed in front of the structural frame.

Promontory Apartments, Chicago, 1946–49

This 22-storey apartment tower stands on the southern stretch of Lake Shore Drive overlooking Lake Michigan.

The structure is of exposed reinforced concrete with brick panels. The reinforced-concrete columns are stepped back progressively towards the upper storeys as the loads decrease. The sketches overleaf record the development: the first drawing shows a concrete version with the brick filled panels; the second shows the application of a steel-and-glass skin. The steel-and-glass version was developed with the intention of giving the interior greater openness and the technique was used in later tower projects.

Promontory Apartments.
Reinforced-concrete version with
columns decreasing in size and
stepped back towards the top of
the building

Steel-and-glass version.
The unfolding of the curtain wall

860 Lake Shore Drive Apartments, Chicago, 1948–51

Lake Shore Drive with its eight traffic lanes runs between the shore of Lake Michigan and these two apartment towers. The towers are set with their long sides at right angles to each other, their orientation being determined by the city road grid.

The 26 apartment floors are carried by a steel skeleton which had to be fireproofed with concrete to conform with building regulations. The columns are placed 21 feet apart in both directions, dividing the narrow side of the rectangular plan into three bays and the long side into five bays.

The structural expression is achieved by making the steel-finished floor beams and the outer columns run flush with the surface of the glass and thus form the outer skin. The I-beam mullions run the full height of the building at 5 ft 3 in. centres.

The contrast between the glass surfaces and the black structure of the skin is underlined by blinds of a uniform pale colour. Floor-to-ceiling glazing, 8 ft 6 in. high, provides an unrestricted view from each apartment. Both towers contain apartments of several rooms arranged on an open plan.

The ground floor is 17 feet high and is completely glazed. Slabs of travertine run through the entrance hall and its surrounds and connect the two buildings.

The two 26-storey apartment towers. The external finish of the buildings is in steel and glass

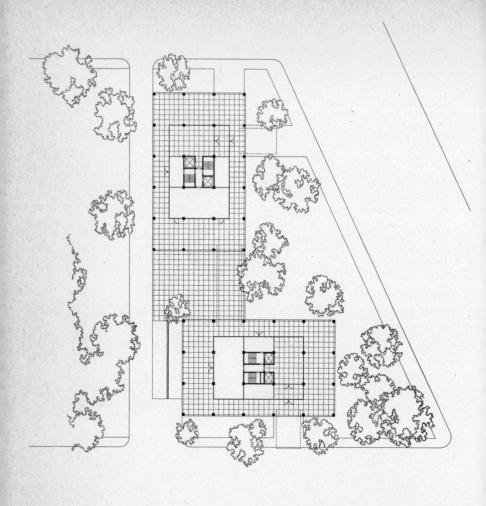

General plan of 860 Lake Shore Drive
Apartments. The expressway and shore of
Lake Michigan are to the right. Scale 1:800

Floor-plan showing uncompromising scheme ▷
for open-plan apartments (not executed).
Scale 1:200

Apartment towers overlooking Lake Michigan:▷▷
860 Lake Shore Drive, and (right) 900 Esplanade
Apartments with curtain walls of grey-tinted
glass

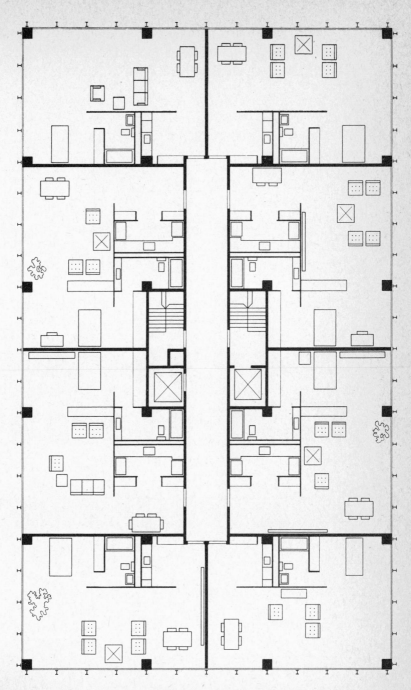

125

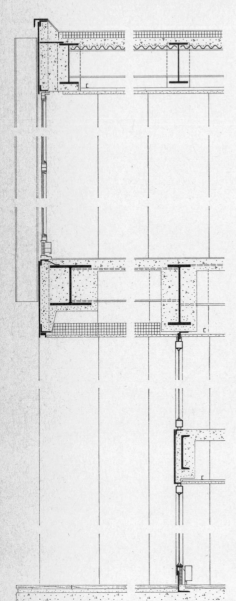

860 Lake Shore Drive: vertical section. Detail showing roof- and floor-slab construction. Scale 1:35

The recessed fully glazed entrance lobby ▷

Detail of the façade showing black-painted ▷▷ steel cladding and curtains and blinds of uniform colour

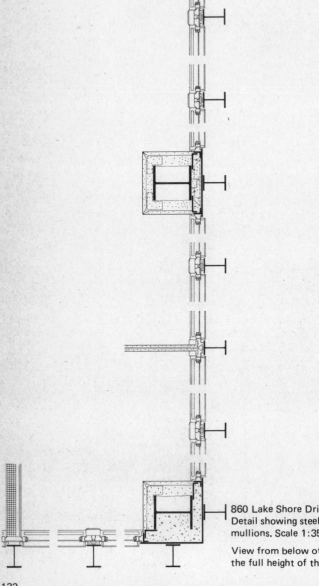

860 Lake Shore Drive: horizontal section.
Detail showing steel cladding and I-beam
mullions. Scale 1:35

View from below of the I-beam mullions running ▷
the full height of the building

Commonwealth Promenade Apartments, Chicago, 1953–56

Economic and air conditioning factors led to further design developments after the 860 Lake Shore Drive Apartment scheme. Since economy dictated the use of reinforced-concrete flat-slab construction a non-load-bearing skin of extruded aluminium and glass was developed to hang in front of the concrete frame. This system of enclosure yields windows of equal size and provides a suitable space between the concrete column and the skin mullions for air conditioning pipes. The columns, which are larger towards the bottom where the load to be borne is greatest, can be seen only from within and do not affect the curtain wall.
Grey tinted glass was used in combination with black aluminium for the 900 Esplanade Apartments (see p. 127) whereas in all the other tower projects the aluminium was left in its natural silver-grey colour.

Corner detail of aluminium curtain walls

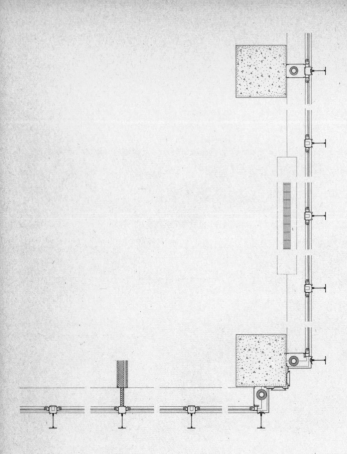

Commonwealth Promenade Apartments:
horizontal section. Detail showing external
cladding attached to reinforced-concrete
columns. Scale 1:50

Detail of curtain wall and cladding in   ▷
aluminium

Steel-framed office buildings with glass curtain wall

The steel-and-glass apartment building now evolved a stage further to produce a new type of office building, a type which has set a trend all over the world.

Mies van der Rohe's remarkable skill in handling the steel-and-glass skeleton allowed him to display his mastery in the rhythmic patterning of the façade and in his use of materials. After the structure has been clarified, attention is turned to the refinements. A particularly good example is provided by the Seagram building, where bronze and tinted glass lend the soaring steel skeleton building a magical effect.

In the low rise offices for Fried. Krupp in Essen and Bacardi in Mexico City, the steel-and-glass structure is articulated with a lively delicacy: the principle of order and regularity permeating the whole is made apparent down to the smallest detail. Nothing is accessory: every detail serves the whole.

Seagram Administration Building, New York, 1954–58

This 39-storey tower block of offices on Park Avenue in the centre of Manhattan's business quarter is set back 90 feet from the Park Avenue building line and soars high above a plaza bounded by the main street and two side streets; the plaza, which is open to the public, is provided with benches on which passers-by can relax. Setting back the building in this way seems to detach it from surrounding structures.

The steel frame of the building is enclosed above the 24-foot-high ground floor by a curtain wall of bronze and bronze-tinted glass. The use of bronze gives the building a striking dignity. The materials on the ground floor are: granite slabs for the floors and terrace, slabs of travertine around the lift shafts, and bronze as an encasement for the columns.

The offices are 9 feet high. The columns are spaced at 28-foot intervals in every direction with 6 window units to each 28-foot bay. Partitions for individual offices can be arranged behind each mullion. The Seagram Administration Building was designed in association with Philip Johnson.

General view of the Seagram Building and its plaza

Block plan showing plaza and siting of building ▷ in relation to Park Avenue at foot. Scale 1:800

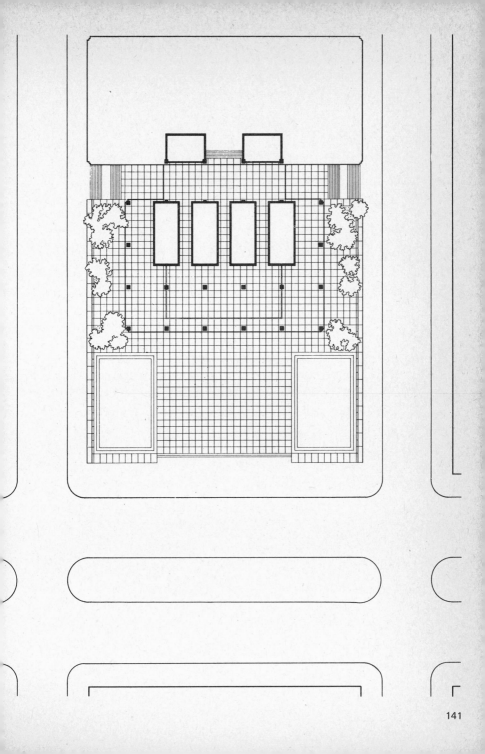

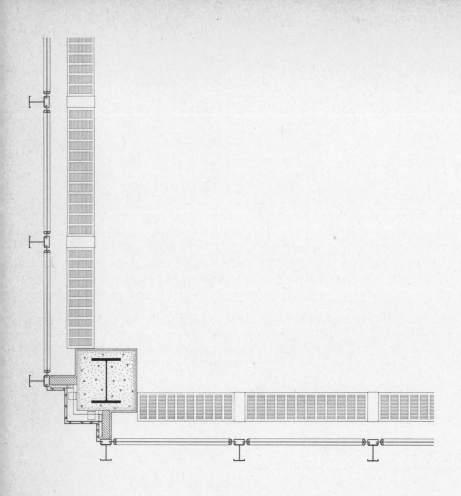

The Seagram Building: horizontal section.
Corner detail showing bronze cladding and
mullions, and air-conditioning grilles.
Scale 1:40

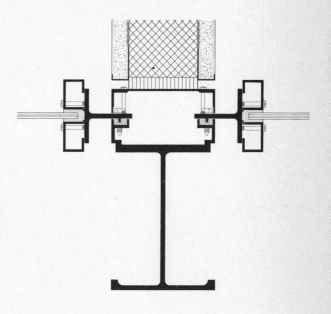

Typical joint showing method of fixing glass
curtain wall. Scale 1:5

Rough sketch of the Seagram plaza with
symmetrically arranged sculptures in foreground

The main entrance and plaza, with service   ▷
building at the rear of the office building

145

Views of the Seagram Building showing bronze cladding and reflective quality of glass curtain walls.

The Seagram Building: entrance lobby with travertine-faced walls and columns encased in bronze

Bacardi Administration Building, Mexico City, 1957–61

The low administration building forms the entrance to the rum distillery of the Bacardi company. It consists of a single-storey hall which is raised 3 metres above ground level so that the body of the building is above the nearby raised highway.

The entrance hall is set back from the façade and completely glazed while, above, the floor of the office storey is opened to form a stair well in the centre. Two symmetrically arranged stairs connect the hall with ground level. Floor and ceiling slabs are supported by exposed columns spaced at intervals of 9 metres in both directions. The total height of the building is 8 metres on a plan measuring 56 x 27 metres. At the narrow ends the office storey is cantilevered 3.5 metres out beyond the last row of columns.

The steel frame and the outer columns are painted black and the floors are of travertine. The enclosing wall is of steel and grey tinted glass. Free-standing panel walls form cores to accommodate the service installations and partition the office spaces on the upper floor.

The central well, with one of the staircases
leading up to the office floor
(see plan overleaf)

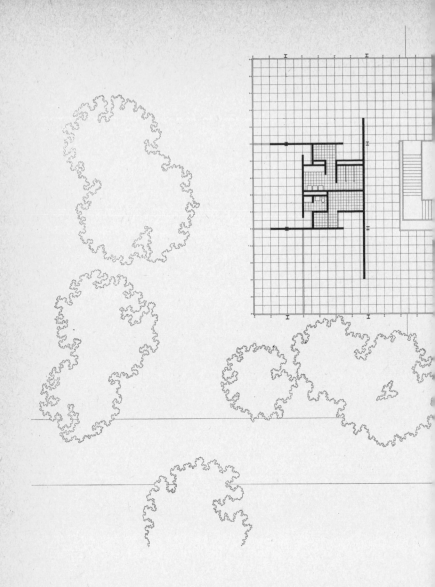

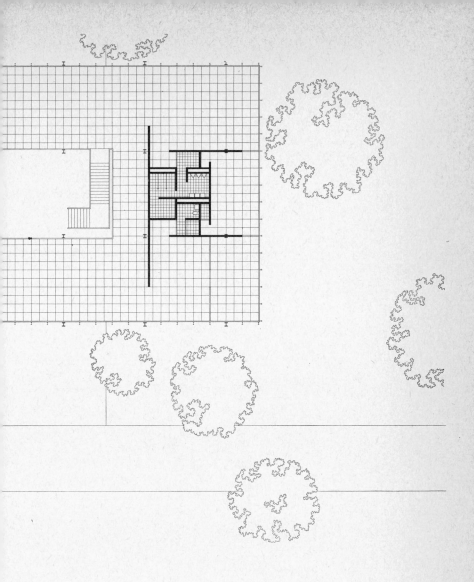

General plan of the Bacardi Administration
Building at first-floor level, showing symmetrical
arrangement and open-plan office areas.
Scale 1:400

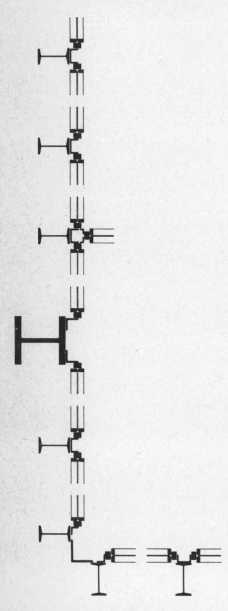

The Bacardi Administration Building:
horizontal section. Detail of curtain wall
construction and supporting column at first-
floor level. Scale 1:25

The glazed recessed entrance lobby paved with▷
travertine slabs

General view showing open-plan offices above▷▷
and enclosed service core at ground level

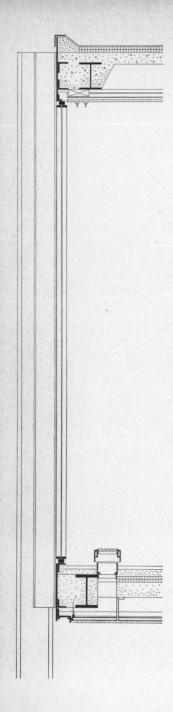

The Bacardi Administration Building:
vertical section. Detail of roof- and floor-slab
construction. Scale 1:35

The exposed steel columns and cantilevered ▷
upper storey

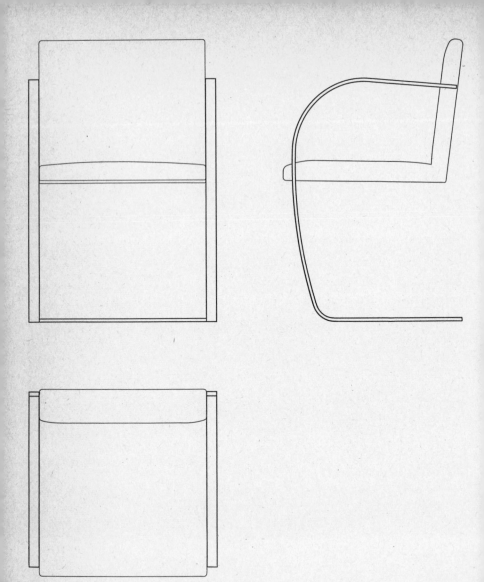

The Brno chair, designed by Mies in 1930.
Scale 1:12.5

The conference room of the Bacardi Admini- ▷
stration Building, with chairs based on the
Brno model

Krupp Administration Building, Essen, Project, 1959–63

A granite-paved terrace on a tree-covered hill forms the base of this building, which has strongly horizontal emphasis. A glazed entrance lobby in the centre of the building connects with the two office floors, which are raised 5 metres above ground level. The ground floor is open and affords views of planted inner courts and of the surrounding countryside. A spacious plaza accents the main entrance on the front. A lower level accommodates restaurants (which open on to outside terraces) and parking and service facilities.

The structure of the building consists of a fireproofed steel frame planned on a 12.80 metre square bay. The skin is of painted steel and grey-tinted plate glass with mullions at 3.20 centres (the building's module). The offices, which are 3.10 metres from floor to ceiling, are planned on either side of a central access corridor. The partitions between offices are designed to be movable.

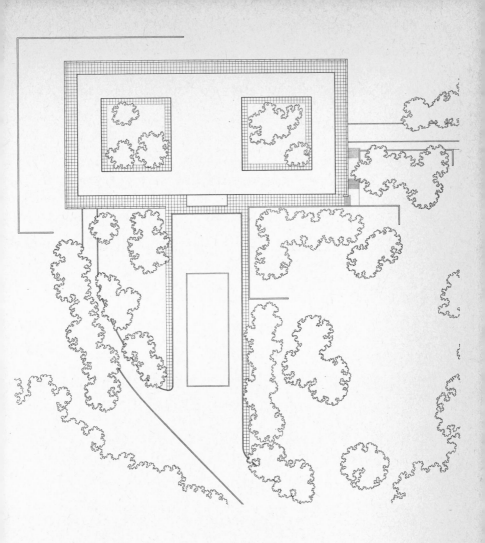

General plan of the project. Scale 1:2,000

General view of a model to show the proposed▷
terrace and open arrangement at ground-floor
level

Town-planning

In these schemes, which embrace single-storey court houses, two-storey row houses and tower blocks, people can find the accommodation best suited to their needs. Mies van der Rohe said: 'Towns are instruments of life. They have to serve life. They are to be measured in terms of life and planned for life.'
A high density of population is unavoidable but living conditions are made tolerable by the introduction of open landscaped areas, Mies van der Rohe's steel-and-glass structures, and above all by a clear layout of circulation routes for all occupants.

Lafayette Park, Detroit 1955—63

The layout of the park was the outcome of a collaboration between Mies van der Rohe and the city planner Ludwig Hilberseimer. Tall apartment towers and one- and two-storey terrace houses form a complete district within a large city. The park has a ring road around it with access roads routed so as to leave a traffic-free zone in the centre as a play and recreation area. Parking areas are below site level.
The reflecting glass surfaces of the terrace houses are almost entirely hidden by the tops of the trees, above which only the apartment towers emerge. By concentrating population in a small site area the apartment towers enable generous stretches of lawn to be left for recreation purposes.

One of the tower blocks overlooking rows of ▷
terrace houses and lawn

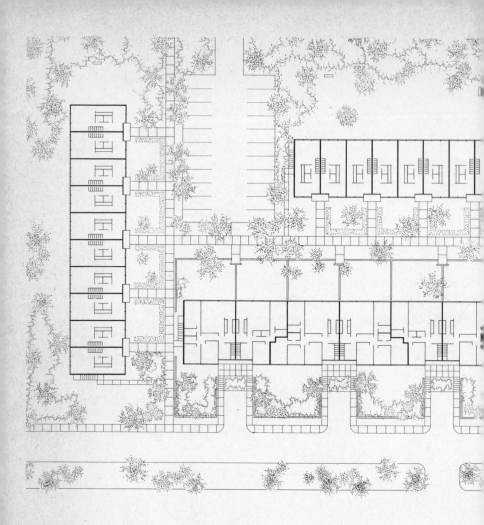

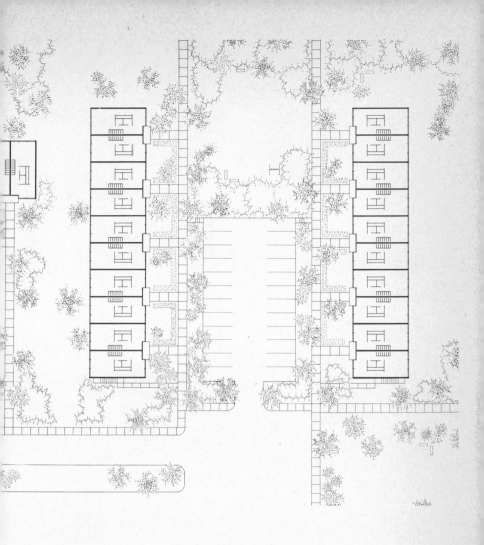

Detail of site plan of Lafayette Park, showing
rows of one- and two-storey terrace houses,
access roads and parking areas. Scale 1:800

Court houses as seen from the apartment ▷▷
towers

The brick wall screening one of the court houses from the open landscaped areas

Row of terrace houses and parking area below ▷ site level

Recreation area between rows of terrace houses ▷ ▷

Hall construction with a wide-span roof

Since structure determined the essential character of a building by Mies
van der Rohe, he could design large-scale buildings which reveal
themselves as masterpieces of engineering and yet display an exquisite
aesthetic sensibility.
A wide-span roof supported only on outside columns yields a free space
in which the creative imagination can be given full play. The freedom
provided by a static structure is the essence of Mies van der Rohe's work.
This 'static' structure is, as it were, the instrument on which his creative
genius could play the 'dynamic' variations of his designs.

Convention Hall, Chicago, project 1953—54

The Convention Hall was planned for a site near the centre of Chicago
within easy reach of all transport facilities. It would be a multi-purpose
hall with seating accommodation for 50,000 persons. A column-free
interior would enable every demand for exhibitions, sports events and
conventions to be met.
The square roof consists of a steel framework unit 30 feet high and
720 feet in span. It rests upon all four outer walls which take the form
of trusses 60 feet in height raised 20 feet above the ground on 6 tapered
concrete columns. The total height of the hall from floor to ceiling
is 110 feet.
The glazed walls of the ground floor are set back 30 feet. Dark grey
marble, aluminium or tinted glass fill the panels so that the structure of
the hall is expressed clearly both inside and outside. Mies always built
in accordance with the principle that 'the construction is the building
itself .

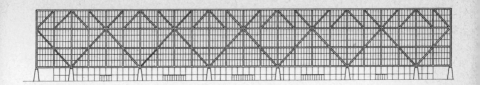

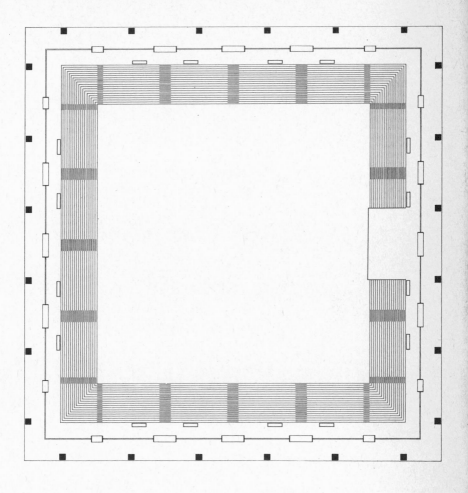

Elevation and plan of the Convention Hall.
Scale 1:2,000

177

Convention Hall, Chicago: detail of vertical section showing roof construction. Scale 1:300

Detail of model showing tapered concrete columns supporting steel framework with infilled panels ▷

Model of the proposed building showing truss▷▷ construction. The facing shown is of marble slabs, an alternative scheme proposed by the architect

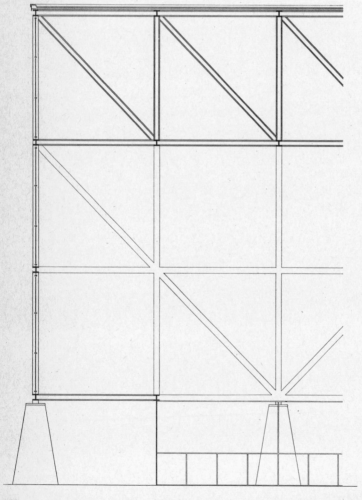

Bacardi Building at Santiago (Cuba), project 1957

The building programme called for a hall of concrete construction
with a column-free interior.
The roof measuring 54 x 54 metres is a rigid 'egg crate' made up of
intersecting concrete beams. At each of its outside edges it is supported
on two concrete columns. In section the columns take the form of a
cross with a 'hinge' at the top to take the weight of the roof. The hall is
7 metres in height and stands on a podium set in the sloping landscape.
The glazed enclosing wall is set back from the roof periphery.

Drawing to illustrate use of concrete column
of cruciform section, with glazed wall set back

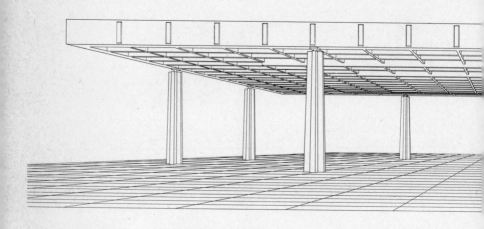

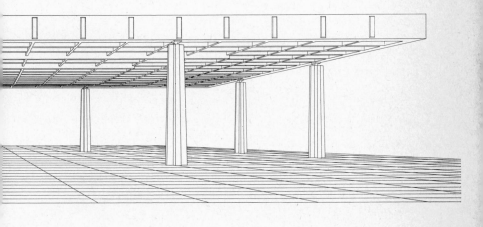

Drawing to illustrate the structure of the
Bacardi Building, with 'egg-crate' roof supported
at each side by two columns

Georg-Schäfer-Museum, Schweinfurt, project 1960

The same construction scheme as for the Santiago project, but now in steel, was proposed for the Georg-Schäfer-Museum in Schweinfurt, and was used for the New National Gallery in West Berlin. For the museum project the design for a rigid square roof plate consisted of welded intersecting girders, supported by eight steel columns of welded T-beams. A suspended acoustic ceiling was proposed in the large glazed hall of the museum.

A great hall can be used for a wide range of purposes, e.g. as an office or for the exhibition of works of art. The fact that intending users proposed to insert a concert hall into the building on a free floor plan irrespective of the structure shows that this type of hall is almost infinitely flexible in the functions it can serve. In size these spacious halls are comparable to the large industrial buildings constructed by engineers: the structural principles have a universal validity.

Detail of model showing roof construction, cruciform steel columns and glazing

New National Gallery, West Berlin, 1962–68

The square glass-enclosed hall for travelling art exhibitions stands on a broad terrace. Beneath the terrace is the gallery for the permanent collection of twentieth-century art, the administration, and storage. The site slopes down to its western end where the terrace forms a walled courtyard which provides daylight for the gallery rooms on the lower floor.

The roof of the hall is a flat, two-directional structure 1.80 metres deep. It consists of welded steel web-girders arranged at 3.60 metre centres in both directions and forming a square structural grid. The continuous plate is reinforced with ribs to prevent buckling. Eight steel columns, two on each side, support the roof. The roof structure measures 64.80 x 64.80 metres and the interior of the hall is 8.40 metres high.

The glazed walls are set back 7.20 metres on all sides so as to leave an arcade between the glass and the columns. The terrace and the floor of the hall are paved with granite slabs measuring 1.20 x 1.20 metres.

At the gallery level the building is a reinforced-concrete structure (columns at intervals of 7.20 metres). The finishes for the gallery rooms (4 metres high) are plaster ceilings painted white, plywood panel walls also painted white, and terrazzo for the floors.

The exhibition hall and museum spaces at the lower level have ceiling lights for general illumination, and in addition the exhibition hall has provision for a number of spotlights which can be inserted in the ceiling wherever needed. A specially designed system was installed to light the picture walls.

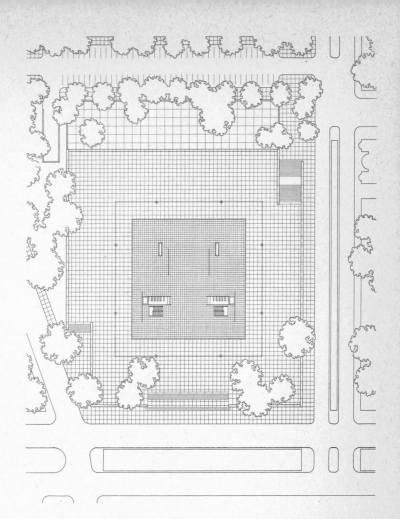

General plan of the New National Gallery.
Scale 1:1,600

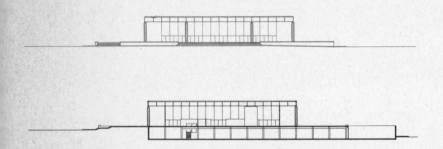

New National Gallery, West Berlin: front
elevation, and sectional drawing showing upper
and lower exhibition areas. Scale 1:1,600

Detail of steel column and roof structure   ▷

General view from the west, with the   ▷▷
Matthiaskirche and Philharmonie (concert
hall, 1963) beyond

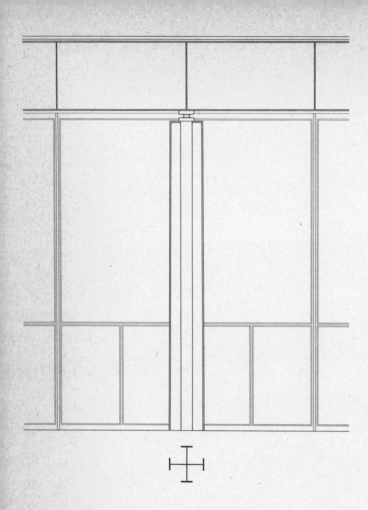

New National Gallery, West Berlin: drawing to
show relationship of vertical and horizontal
steel members, and (below) section of cruciform
column Scale 1:100

Interior with groups of Barcelona chairs; the ▷
floor is paved with granite slabs

Biography

1886	29 March, Ludwig Mies van der Rohe born at Aachen
1897–1900	Attended the Domschule at Aachen
1900–02	Pupil at the Aachen Trade School Worked in his father's stonemason's business
1902	Trainee on building sites
1903–04	Draughtsman working on stucco ornaments in a stucco business
1905–07	Furniture designer with Bruno Paul in Berlin
1908–11	Architect with Peter Behrens in Berlin
1912–37	Own architect's practice in Berlin
1921–25	Organizer of exhibitions for November Group
1926	In charge of the Werkbund Exhibition 'The Dwelling' Weissenhof development at Stuttgart
1926–32	Vice-president of the German Werkbund
1929	Creator of the building representing Germany at the World Exhibition in Barcelona
1930–33	Director of the Bauhaus at Dessau and Berlin
1931	Head of the Werkbund section 'The Dwelling of our Time' at the Berlin Building Exhibition
1938–58	Director of the School of Architecture of the Illinois Institute of Technology, Chicago. Replanning of campus

1938	Own architect's practice in Chicago
1948	First curtain wall of steel and glass in the apartment towers in Chicago
1950	Development of column-free interiors in hall constructions with wide-span roofs
1959	Member of the Order Pour le Mérite (Federal Republic of Germany) Distinctions and honours in Europe and USA
1963	Presidential Medal of Freedom, conferred by the President of the United States
1969	17 August, Mies van der Rohe died in Chicago

Buildings and projects by Mies van der Rohe

1907	Riehl House, Berlin-Neubabelsberg, Germany
1911	Perls House, Berlin-Zehlendorf, Germany (later Fuchs House)
1912	Project: Kröller House, The Hague, The Netherlands Project: Bismarck Monument, Bingen, Germany
1913	House on the Heerstrasse, Berlin, Germany
1914	Urbig House, Berlin-Neubabelsberg, Germany Project: House for the Architect, Werder, Germany (two versions)
1919	Project: Kempner House, Berlin, Germany
1920–21	Project: Glass skyscraper
1921	Kempner House, Berlin, Germany (destroyed) Project: Office Building, Friedrichstrasse, Berlin, Germany Project: Petermann House, Berlin-Neubabelsberg, Germany
1922	Project: Concrete office building, Berlin, Germany Project: Concrete country house Project: Lessing House, Berlin-Neubabelsberg, Germany Project: Eliat House, Nedlitz, near Potsdam, Germany
1923	Project: Brick country house
1924	Mosler House, Berlin-Neubabelsberg, Germany Project: Traffic Tower, Berlin, Germany
1925–26	Wolf House, Guben, Germany
1926	Monument to Karl Liebknecht and Rosa Luxemburg, Berlin, Germany (destroyed)
1926–27	Municipal Housing Development, Afrikanischestrasse, Berlin, Germany
1927	Werkbund Exposition, Weissenhofsiedlung, Stuttgart, Germany Apartment Building, Weissenhofsiedlung, Stuttgart, Germany Silk Exhibit, Exposition de la Mode, Berlin, Germany (with Lilly Reich)
1928	Addition to Fuchs House (Perls House), Berlin-Zehlendorf, Germany Hermann Lange House, Krefeld, Germany (badly damaged) Esters House, Krefeld, Germany (badly damaged) Project: Remodelling of Alexanderplatz, Berlin, Germany Project: Adam Building, Leipzigerstrasse, Berlin, Germany Project: Bank building, Stuttgart, Germany
1928–29	German Pavilion, International Exposition, Barcelona, Spain (demolished) Electricity Pavilion, International Exposition, Barcelona, Spain (demolished) Industrial Exhibits, International Exposition, Barcelona, Spain (with Lilly Reich)
1928–30	Tugendhat House, Brno, Czechoslovakia (badly damaged)
1929	Project: Office Building, Friedrichstrasse, Berlin, Germany (second scheme)
1930	Apartment interior, New York, N.Y. Project: Country Club, Krefeld, Germany Project: War Memorial, Berlin, Germany Project: Gericke House, Wannsee, Berlin, Germany
1931	House, Berlin Building Exposition, Berlin, Germany (demolished) Apartment for a bachelor, Berlin Building Exposition, Berlin, Germany (demolished)

1931	Projects: Court houses
1932	Lemcke House, Berlin, Germany
1933	Factory Building and Power House for the Silk Industry, Vereinigte Seiden-webereien AG, Krefeld, Germany Project: Reichsbank, Berlin, Germany
1934	Mining Exhibits, Deutsches Volk, Deutsche Arbeit, Exposition, Berlin, Germany Project: House for the Architect, Tyrol, Austria Project: German Pavilion, International Exposition, Brussels, Belgium Project: Service station
1935	Project: Ulrich Lange House, Krefeld, Germany (two versions) Project: Hubbe House, Magdeburg, Germany
1937	Project: Administration Building for the Silk Industry, Vereinigte Seiden-webereien AG, Krefeld, Germany
1938	Project: Resor House, Jackson Hole, Wyoming
1939	Preliminary campus plan, Illinois Institute of Technology, Chicago, Illinois
1940–41	Master plan, Illinois Institute of Technology, Chicago, Illinois
1942	Project: Museum for a Small City Project: Concert Hall
1942–43	Metals Research Building for Armour Research Foundation, Illinois Institute of Technology Research Institute, Chicago, Illinois (Associate Architects: Holabird and Root)
1944	Project: Library and Administration Building, Illinois Institute of Technology, Chicago, Illinois
1944–46	Engineering Research Building for Armour Research Foundation, Illinois Institute of Technology Research Institute, Chicago, Illinois (Associate Architects: Holabird and Root)
1945	Studies for Classroom Buildings, Illinois Institute of Technology, Chicago, Illinois Project: Mooringsport Power Station, Mooringsport, Louisiana Meredosia Power Station, Meredosia, Louisiana Havana Power Station, Havana, Illinois (with Sargent and Lundy, Engineers)
1945–46	Alumni Memorial Hall, Illinois Institute of Technology, Chicago, Illinois (Associate Architects: Holabird and Root) Perlstein Hall (Metallurgical and Chemical Engineering Building), Illinois Institute of Technology, Chicago, Illinois (Associate Architects: Holabird and Root) Wishnick Hall (Chemistry Building), Illinois Institute of Technology, Chicago, Illinois (Associate Architects: Friedman, Alschuler and Sincere) Project: Cantor Drive-In Restaurant, Indianapolis, Indiana
1945–50	Fox River House (Farnsworth House), Plano, Illinois Boiler Plant, Illinois Institute of Technology, Chicago, Illinois
1946–47	Project: Cantor House, Indianapolis, Indiana
1946–49	Promontory Apartments, Chicago, Illinois (Associate Architects: Pace Associates, and Holsman, Holsman, Klekamp and Taylor)
1947	Central Vault, Illinois Institute of Technology, Chicago, Illinois Project: Theatre

1947	Project: Gymnasium and Swimming Pool, Illinois Institute of Technology, Chicago, Illinois
1947–50	Institute of Gas Technology, Illinois Institute of Technology, Chicago, Illinois (Associate Architects: Friedman, Alschuler and Sincere)
1948	Project: Student Union Building, Illinois Institute of Technology, Chicago, Illinois
1948–50	Association of American Railroads Administration Building, Illinois Institute of Technology, Chicago, Illinois (Associate Architects: Friedman, Alschuler and Sincere)
1948–51	860 and 880 Lake Shore Drive Apartments, Chicago, Illinois (Associate Architects: Pace Associates, and Holsman, Holsman, Klekamp and Taylor) Interior, The Arts Club of Chicago, Chicago, Illinois Project: Algonquin Apartments, Chicago, Illinois (two versions)
1948–53	Mechanical Engineering Building for the Association of American Railroads, Illinois Institute of Technology, Chicago, Illinois (Associate Architects: Friedman, Alschuler and Sincere)
1949–50	Project: Cantor Commercial Center Office Building, Indianapolis, Indiana
1949–52	Chapel, Illinois Institute of Technology, Chicago, Illinois
1950	Project: Caine House, Winnetka, Illinois Project: Dormitory and Fraternity House, Illinois Institute of Technology, Chicago, Illinois
1950–56	Crown Hall (Architecture, City Planning and Design Building), Illinois Institute of Technology, Chicago, Illinois (Associate Architects: Pace Associates)
1950–51	Project: Steel Frame Prefabricated Row House Project: Fifty Foot by Fifty Foot House
1950–52	Mechanical Engineering Research Building I, Illinois Institute of Technology Research Institute, Chicago, Illinois (Associate Architects: Friedman, Alschuler and Sincere) Project: Berke Office Building, Indianapolis, Indiana
1951–52	McCormick House, Elmhurst, Illinois Project: Pi Lamda Phi Fraternity House, Bloomington, Indiana
1951–53	Carman Hall, Illinois Institute of Technology, Chicago, Illinois (Associate Architects: Pace Associates)
1952–53	Commons Building, Illinois Institute of Technology, Chicago, Illinois (Associate Architects: Friedman, Alschuler and Sincere) Project: National Theatre, Mannheim, Germany
1952–55	Cunningham Hall, Illinois Institute of Technology, Chicago, Illinois (Associate Architects: Pace Associates) Bailey Hall, Illinois Institute of Technology, Chicago, Illinois (Associate Architects: Pace Associates)
1953–54	Project: Convention Hall, Chicago, Illinois
1953–56	Commonwealth Promenade Apartments, Chicago, Illinois (Associate Architects: Friedman, Alschuler and Sincere) 900 Esplanade Apartments, Chicago, Illinois (Associate Architects: Friedman, Alschuler and Sincere)
1954	Master plan for the Museum of Fine Arts, Houston, Texas

1954–58	Seagram Building, 375 Park Avenue, New York, N.Y. (In Association with Philip Johnson, Associate Architects: Kahn and Jacobs) Cullinan Hall, The Museum of Fine Arts, Houston, Texas (Associate Architects: Staub, Rather and Howze)
1955	Project: Lubin Apartment-Hotel, New York, N.Y.
1955–56	Master plan for Lafayette Park, housing project, Detroit, Michigan
1955–57	Association of American Railroads Laboratory Building, Illinois Institute of Technology, Chicago, Illinois (Associate Architects: Friedman, Alschuler and Sincere) Physics-Electronics Research Building, Illinois Institute of Technology Research Institute, Chicago, Illinois (Associate Architects: Naess & Murphy)
1956–58	Metals Research Building, Illinois Institute of Technology Research Institute, Chicago, Illinois (Associate Architects: Holabird and Root)
1957	Project: United States Consulate, São Paulo, Brazil Project: Quadrangles Apartments, Brooklyn, New York Project: Bacardi Office Building, Santiago de Cuba, Cuba Project: Kaiser Office Building, Chicago, Illinois Project: Commercial Building, Pratt Institute, Brooklyn, New York
1957–58	Project: Battery Park Apartment Development, New York, N.Y.
1957–61	Bacardi Office Building, Mexico City, Mexico (Associate Architects: Saenz-Cancio-Martin-Gutierrez)
1958	Pavilion Apartments, Lafayette Park, Detroit, Michigan Town Houses, Lafayette Park, Detroit, Michigan
1958–59	Project: Seagram Office Building, Chicago, Illinois
1958–60	Pavilion Apartments and Colonnade Apartments, Colonnade Park, Newark, New Jersey
1959	Project: Mies van der Rohe Exhibition for V Bienal Exhibit, São Paulo, Brazil
1959–63	Project: Friedrich Krupp Administration Building, Essen, Germany
1959–64	Chicago Federal Center, U.S. Courthouse and Federal Office and U.S. Post Office Building (Joint Venture: Schmidt, Garden & Erikson, Mies van der Rohe, C.F. Murphy Associates, and A. Epstein & Sons, Inc.)
1960–61	Project: Schäfer Museum, Schweinfurt, Germany
1960–63	Home Federal Savings and Loan Association of Des Moines, Des Moines, Iowa (Associate Architects: Smith-Vorhees-Jenson) One Charles Center, office building, Baltimore, Maryland 2400 Lakeview Apartment Building, Chicago, Illinois (Associate Architects: Greenberg and Finfer)
1961	Project: Mountain Place, Montreal, Quebec
1962–65	Social Service Administration Building, The University of Chicago, Chicago, Illinois Meredith Memorial Hall, Drake University, Des Moines, Iowa
1962–68	New National Gallery, West Berlin, Germany The Science Center, Duquesne University, Pittsburgh, Pennsylvania
1963	Lafayette Towers, Lafayette Park, Detroit, Michigan
1963–65	Highfield House, apartment building, Baltimore, Maryland

1963–69	Toronto-Dominion Centre, Toronto, Ontario (John B. Parkin Associates and Bregman and Hamann, Architects; Mies van der Rohe, Consulting Architect)
1965–68	Westmount Square, Montreal, Quebec (Resident Architects: Greenspoon, Freedlander, Plachta & Kryton)
1966	Project: Church Street South K-4 School, New Haven, Connecticut Project: Foster City, apartment buildings, San Mateo, California District of Columbia Public Library, Washington, D.C.
1966–69	Project: Houston Museum Addition, Houston, Texas
1967	Mansion House Square Project, London, England (In association with William Holford and Partners) I.B.M. Regional Office Building, Chicago, Illinois (Joint Venture with C.F. Murphy Associates)
1967–68	Esso Service Station, Nuns' Island, Montreal, Quebec (Resident Architect: Paul LaPointe)
1967–69	High Rise Apartment Building No. 1, Nuns' Island, Montreal, Quebec (Resident Architect: Philip Bobrow) Project: King Broadcasting Studios, Seattle, Washington
1967–70	111 East Wacker Drive, Illinois Central Air Rights Development, Chicago, Illinois
1968	Project: Commerzbank AG, office building and bank, Frankfurt/Main, Germany
1968–69	High Rise Apartment Buildings No. 2 and 3, Nuns' Island, Montreal, Quebec (Resident Architect: Edgar Tornay) Project: Northwest Plaza Project, Chicago, Illinois Project: Dominion Square Project, Montreal, Quebec

Buildings and projects by the Office of Mies van der Rohe, since 1969
Partners: Joseph Fujikawa, Bruno Conterato, Dirk Lohan
Associates: John Bowman, Peter Carter, Douglas Johnson, Gerald Johnson, Arthur Salzmann

1969	Project: Vereinigte Glaswerke, Aachen, Germany
1969–70	Project: Indiana Bell Telephone Company, District Office and T.S.P.S., Columbia, Indiana
1969	High Rise Apartment Building No. 4, Nuns' Island, Montreal, Quebec American Life and Accident Insurance Company of Kentucky, Office Building, Louisville, Kentucky Two Illinois Center Office Building, Chicago, Illinois Master Plan, Illinois Central Air Rights Development, Chicago, Illinois (In collaboration with Solomon, Cordwell, Buenz & Associates) The Loop College, City Colleges of Chicago, Chicago, Illinois (Joint venture with J.W. Sih & Associates)
1970	Tuley High School, Chicago, Illinois Orr High School, Chicago, Illinois

Acknowledgments

It was a great privilege for me to work with Ludwig Mies van der Rohe in the preparation of this book; his untiring and sympathetic assistance was matched by his generosity in providing me with valuable original material. My grateful thanks are extended to his associates of many years' standing for their unfailing helpfulness, their advice and their corrections, in particular Dirk Lohan and Gene Summers, and John Fleming who made the line drawings.

I should like to thank the Museum of Modern Art in New York for their courtesy in loaning drawings and collages (36–37, 40–41, 48–49, 52–53, 75–79), the George Danforth private collection for a charcoal sketch (16–17), Phyllis Lambert for a pencil sketch (144), and James Speyer for a pen-and-ink sketch (43). My grateful thanks to Ogden Hannaford and Myron Goldsmith, with whom I stayed during the summer months of 1963 and 1964. The original idea of planning the book I owe to Eduard Neuenschwander and Christian Norberg Schulz. My special thanks to my friends who had a hand in the making of the book and helped me to reduce it to its essentials: Lucius Burckhardt, Antonio Hernandez, Adolf Jacob and Friedrich Störk.

I should also like to thank the Museum of Modern Art in New York for kindly placing at my disposal negatives of the earlier buildings in Germany; Hedrich Blessing for the photographs of models (85, 164–165, 179–181, 187); and Jane Doggett and Malcolm Smith for a photograph (140). All other photographs were provided by the publisher.

W.B., Basle, 1964 and 1971